# DJ Sound Hound's Dance Party

## An Onomatopoeia Concert

Written by Stacy J. Shaneyfelt

Illustrated by Yago Soares

# Dedication Page

I lovingly dedicate this book to all the teachers who make grammar and literacy a daily "dance party" with their amazing lessons. Thank you for sharing our tunes and talents, especially Carrie, Shannon, Ivana, Higs, Sam, Dray, and Kam, true masters of instruction and music of the heart!

Are you ready to woof and yelp with DJ Sound Hound today? He'll surely pop, drop, and bark beats in a smashing way!

Discover some amusing onomatopoeias during this guessing game in fur: Listen for words like giggle, wiggle, howl, plop, and purr!

Again, find words that imitate the sounds they represent. DJ Sound Hound will offer onomatopoeias from his doggy tent!

SOUND HOUND

HOUND

DJSH

First of all, he blares Halsey Hen's new hit song. Clucks, cackles, and chirps keep the jams strong.

Which backup singers make these special tweets? Point to them now before they flee with webbed feet.

Next, spot the crew that meows, moos, and cock-a-doodle-doos?

How about the others that quack, whack, and smack too?

PEARL CLAM

Suddenly, the crowd ahhs and claps for the next hip hop jam. Zap, tap, and rap with this oinker before he becomes ham!

Then with a boom, vroom, and zoom, this puffing bad boy blares and bellows. Who really knew that he was one of country music's most talented fellows?

Immediately after, this crazy act features Kacey Muskrat, Bat Bryan, and Turkey McGraw. They bobble, wobble, and gobble performances that are totally off the wall!

So guess who toots, scoots, and hoots in the next galloping group? Neigh, bray, and munch all day-not to mention scoop!

As sunset sweeps in, all the stomping,
romping, and chomping slows,
It's time to wow, pow, and growl with

onomatopoeias

on your own, you know.
How many total did you locate
during this dance party today?
Count and practice them
in your own genre or way!

# Bonus/Post-Reading Activities, Family Fun, and Animal Adventures

**-Humor Heals-**
Which piece of art is the most humorous from this book? Why? What appeals to you the most? Let humor heal!

**-Zoo Crew-**
Think of 4-6 zoo animals from A to Z. Play a drawing, charades, or guessing game to showcase their onomatopeias. Buzz with creativity!

**-Rhyme Climbs-**
The author uses poetry and rhyme to make the text musical. Locate 2-4 pairs of rhyming words from the book. Recite them aloud to perfect your speech skills!

**-Picture Perfect-**
Make a picture, a PowerPoint presentation, or a collage of 4-6 of your favorite onomatopoeias from this book. Be creative!

**-Math Matters-**
Scan the book again and count all the onomatopeias. How many did the author use overall?

# Bonus/Post-Reading Activities, Family Fun, and Animal Adventures

**-Word Wisdom-**

Using context clues, define 4-6 new vocabulary words from the book.

**-Pet Spotters-**

Are you an animal lover? Name a bird, a mammal, and a mollusk from the book.

**-Music Master-**

There are some musical references in the names of the members and bands of DJ Sound Hound's party. Can you spot 3 of them?

**-Soar With Science-**

Walk, hike, bike, or sit in nature. Record 4-6 onomatopoeias that you hear.

**-Genre Jet-**

Make a jet or an airplane and decorate it with 4-5 genres of your favorite music. For example, I like pop, rock, New Age, hip hop, and Broadway genres.

# Free Gift: Onomatopoeia Practice Doodle Page

WOOF!

Doodle or draw which animals make the following onomatopeias. You can also use clay, collage materials, or any crafting supplies with an adult's supervision and permission.

1. purr

2. chirp

3. moo

4. neigh

5. yelp

# ABOUT THE AUTHOR

After obtaining her BS in Secondary English Education and MA in English from Slippery Rock University of PA, Stacy embarked on a successful teaching career that spanned public, government, and charter schools in Pittsburgh, PA, Oklahoma City, Norman, OK, and Okinawa, Japan. She proudly earned a 2004 Fulbright-Hays Seminar Scholarship to Thailand and Vietnam, Teacher of the Year in two schools, and directed many plays and performances.

In addition to multicultural and social activism, Stacy now savors sweet moments with her awesome husband, two fierce and fabulous daughters, and three frisky fur babies. Presently works as a virtual freelancer, a private English and ESL tutor, and an online editor/proofreader, She enjoys films, travel, coffee, art, and all things mindful!

# ABOUT THE ARTIST

Yago is a young Brazillian artist that loves mystical and whimsical scenarios. In his early youth, he attended to the Edson Muniz Art Academy, specializing in Western and Eastern comics, as well as watercolor painting. After being mesmerized by Aaron Blaise and Bobby Chiu's work, Yago started his journey specializing in digital art, attending to art conventions and taking many digital art courses. Presently, he is pursuing a Bachelor and Licentiate degree in Visual Arts at UNESP – São Paulo State University, Brazil.

Yago works as a freelance Art Teacher and Illustrator. He loves to learn more about Biology and History and some of his hobbies include tending to his plants and pets, playing and listening to music, and discovering new recipes to cook!

Thank you for buying this book.
As a working mom and military
spouse, your reviews mean so much
to me because I aim to unite global
readers through art and literacy.
Kindly post a short review
on this book's Amazon page. I truly
appreciate this book buzz with me!
If you like this book, then
please browse my other offerings today!

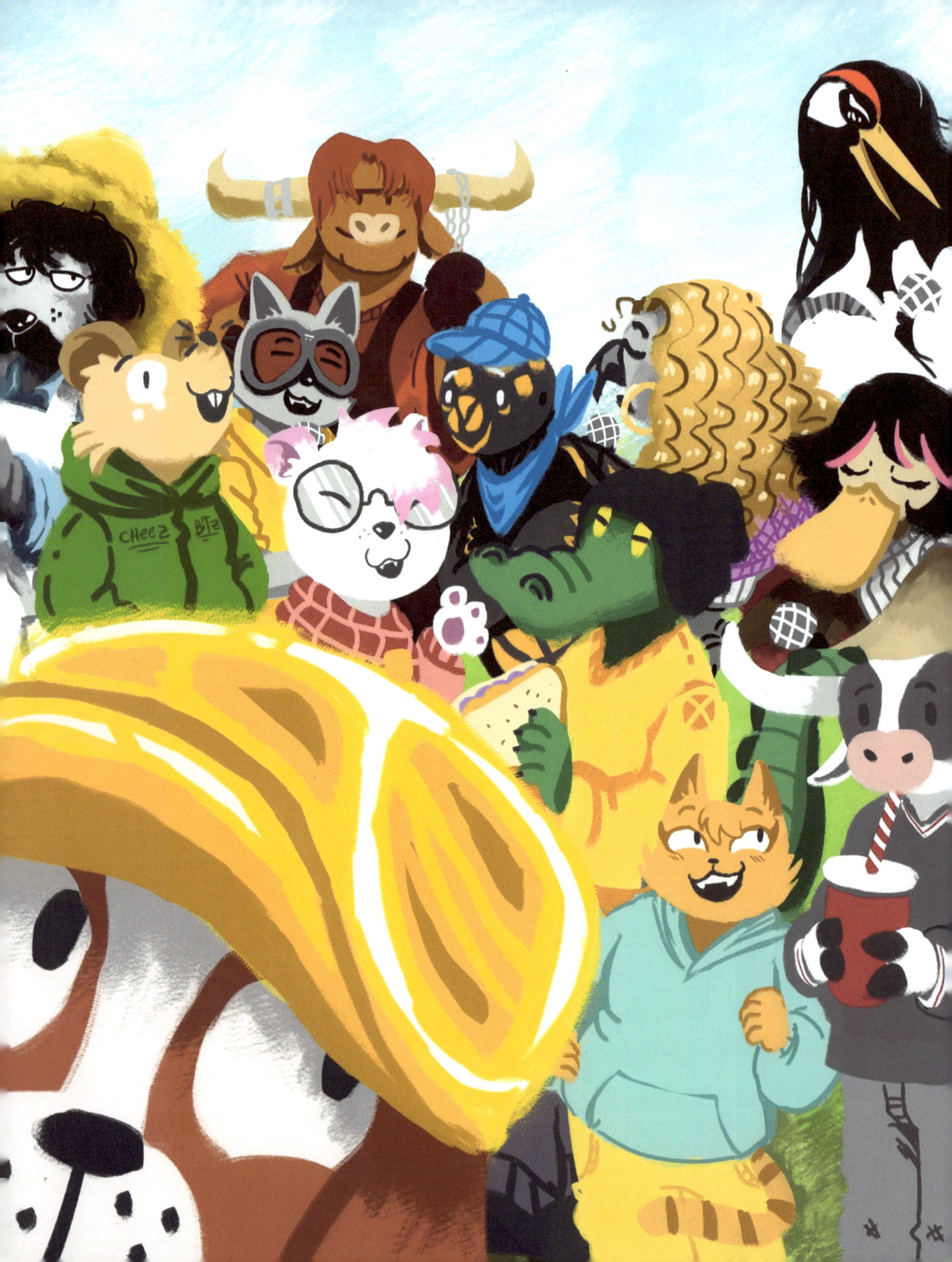
CHeeZ
BITZ

www.ingramcontent.com/pod-product-compliance
Lightning Source LLC
Chambersburg PA
CBHW040024050426
42452CB00002B/125